Original title:
Life's Purpose: Still Not Sure

Copyright © 2025 Creative Arts Management OÜ
All rights reserved.

Author: Julian Prescott
ISBN HARDBACK: 978-1-80566-269-3
ISBN PAPERBACK: 978-1-80566-564-9

The Color of Uncertainty

In the whirl of doubt, I walk the line,
Chasing answers wrapped in a twine.
Socks mismatched, like my thoughts today,
Is it bright blue, or just shades of gray?

I asked my cat about the way,
He blinked and napped, so I can't say.
The coffee brews while I ponder fate,
Maybe it's time to just clean my plate!

Google's my friend, so I browse online,
Found a guru with a neon sign.
"Follow your heart," the wisdom said,
But my heart just wants to sleep instead.

So here I sit, a jester in doubt,
With spaghetti thoughts that are all turned about.
If laughter's the goal, then I've hit a score,
Uncertainty's fun—who could ask for more?

A Canvas of Possibilities

With every brush, I change my mind,
Is this Picasso, or a new kind?
Splashes of orange where green should go,
Artistic chaos? A definite show!

The canvas waits, a blank stare back,
I ponder my skills, or lack thereof, a knack.
Dancing with colors, not sure where to land,
My palette's a party, oh so unplanned!

A squirrel's my muse, with acorn in tow,
Inspiration strikes, then quickly goes.
Sometimes a swirl, other times a dot,
Abstract confusion? I think I've got!

So in this swirl of hues and shades,
Each line of my tale adeptly fades.
I laugh with the brush, as it strokes and slips,
Maybe my purpose is just making quips!

Shadows of Purpose

In search of meaning, I tripped on a shoe,
Who knew my true calling was to wear it askew?
The universe chuckled, pointing with glee,
"Just embrace the absurd, it's all part of thee."

I asked a wise sage, 'What's my grand quest?'
He offered me snacks, said, 'Chill, take a rest!'
So I pondered the chips while I munched with delight,
Maybe purpose is nachos, all warm and just right.

Threads of Introspection

I knitted my thoughts on a whimsical spree,
Lost half my yarn; it unraveled with glee.
The needles got tangled, a mess that I made,
Perhaps life's a sweater that I need to trade.

I found a lost sock, it had secrets to share,
It whispered of lost dreams, told them with flair.
So I wear mismatched shoes, and I color outside,
Maybe purpose is laughter, a joy-filled ride.

Tentative Steps

I tiptoed through life on my tippy-tip toes,
Tripped over a garden of thorny red rose.
I tried to find answers, I wrote them in chalk,
But the wind washed them away—guess it's just talk!

With every step forward, I danced like a fool,
Fell into puddles while breaking the rule.
But who knew the silliness sprouted like trees?
In this silly old waltz, I found purpose with ease.

Glimmers of Insight

A light bulb flickered; I jumped in surprise,
Was it wisdom or bugs? They're crafty, the lies!
I fumbled with matches, tried lighting the way,
But the fire took flight, just like a cliché.

As I chased down the spark with a grin on my face,
I realized that humor can lighten the race.
Perhaps in the chaos, there's joy to ignite,
In giggles and chuckles, our purpose takes flight.

A Compass of Doubt

I bought a compass, quite the find,
It points to places, but none unwind.
North is a mystery, south's a jest,
Where's the map to this unwritten quest?

I spin in circles, round and round,
With each step forward, I lose ground.
Maybe just dance, let fate decide,
Or grab some snacks for this wild ride.

Echoes of Ambivalence

In the morning I wake, and what do I dread?
Choosing cereal or toast for breakfast spread.
With choices aplenty, I ponder and pause,
Is this how I'll spend my eternal cause?

Flipping a coin for a life-altering stake,
Heads, I go for coffee; tails, I just bake.
Would a clear answer actually be in sight?
Or is it just chaos wrapped up in delight?

The Quest for Clarity

Set out on a journey, a hero am I,
In search of a reason, oh where, oh why?
Maps are confusing, should I trust my gut?
I found a taco truck — oh, what a cut!

Philosophers ponder, I just crave fries,
Drowning in thought, with snacks as my prize.
Is clarity waiting at the end of the road?
Or just another detour where laughter's bestowed?

Reflections in a Fog

Walking through fog, I squint and I stare,
Is it my reflection or just thin air?
With each step I shuffle, the ground feels unsteady,
Do I trust my senses, or be more ready?

Misty decisions confuse my headspace,
Is this just a phase or my rightful place?
Laughter is fleeting, like shadows at dawn,
Guess I'll tackle tomorrow with pancakes and brawn.

When Every Step Feels Heavy

Each morning greets me like a brick,
But I still pretend I'm spry and quick.
The coffee pot glares, 'You need a plan!'
Yet my goals scatter like grains of sand.

I wander through tasks with a sleepy grin,
Wondering where my motivation has been.
The weight of my dreams feels like a stone,
Perhaps I'll just sit here, all on my own.

Yet somewhere, a laugh rings true in the air,
Reminding me life is a peculiar affair.
With each floppy step and misplaced shoe,
I chuckle, because what else can you do?

So I dance with my doubts, a wobbly sway,
Proving each stumble can brighten the day.
When every step feels like lifting a cow,
I'll simply laugh and stretch, as best as I know how.

Symphony of Unanswered Whys

I ponder the purpose of socks, quite lost,
Two go into the dryer, but what's the cost?
Do they plot an escape to a land of fluff?
Or is it a fabric war? It's just too tough!

With questions like butterflies, flitting about,
I chase after answers, but that's what I doubt.
Why do we do the things that we do?
Maybe I'm meant to just follow the skew.

While deep thoughts tumble like tumbleweeds,
My mind takes a detour, it rarely concedes.
Perhaps a sandwich holds wisdom profound,
Or the color of jelly makes logic unbound.

This symphony plays, and oh what a sound,
With unanswered whys that forever abound.
In laughter's embrace, I twirl and I fly,
Unearthing delight in each curious why.

The Art of Wandering Thought

I set out to conquer my day with a map,
But wind gusts strike hard, and I take a nap.
Each thought that I chase seems to ride on a kite,
I follow its tail, losing sense of the fight.

The art of distraction, a skill I possess,
Where focus escapes like a hamster in stress.
I meant to write down a grocery list,
But instead, I wrote sonnets—am I that off the twist?

With coffee in hand, I plan my grand schemes,
Yet I'm sidetracked by daydreams of pizza and creams.
What was I meant to accomplish today?
Oh well, let's just order, and take it away.

So here I remain, in a whirl of delight,
Where thoughts come to dance in a curious flight.
The art of wandering, a joyous parade,
In the circus of life, we all pirouette unmade.

Beneath the Weight of Wonder

Under the sky of what-ifs and coulds,
I ponder existence in my mismatched goods.
Each moment is heavy, like lifting a cat,
Why does it weigh so much? I'll take a nap, stat!

In fields full of questions, I often lay low,
Wrestling with thoughts, like a circus of woe.
Do I need a purpose, or just a good snack?
Perhaps the answer is to just play hacky sack!

With every dilemma shaped like a pie,
I slice it with laughter, asking just why.
Under the weight of my jumbled delight,
I find joy in nonsense that tickles the night.

So let's raise a toast to the wonders we bear,
To friends and to laughter that dance in the air.
Beneath all our worries, we giggle and play,
Finding comfort together in a whimsical way.

Glimmers in the Fog

I wander through the morning mist,
With coffee stains upon my wrist.
A map is nice, but who's to say,
Which road is right? I lost my way.

The sun peeks out, it plays a trick,
That shiny bridge? It's just a stick!
I chase my shadow, think it's won,
But wait, it seems we're having fun!

The fog rolls in, my thoughts collide,
I trip and fall, no one can hide.
A giggle here, a stutter there,
Who knew the path was filled with air?

I laugh aloud, my head's a mess,
Yet joy, I find, in all the stress.
The road may twist and turn unkind,
But hey, at least I've got my mind!

Uncharted Waters of Existence

I'm sailing on a boat, it rocks,
My compass spins, I check my socks.
What's that ahead? A floating shoe,
Or just my dreams? I've lost a few.

The ocean laughs, it swells with glee,
A jellyfish winks at me with glee.
I steer with style, or maybe luck,
And wonder how I got this stuck.

Fish jump high, they dance, they play,
"Is that my purpose?" I might say.
But fish don't care, they swim and dive,
Maybe I should just take a drive.

In waves I find a splash of joy,
With every wave, I'm still a kid's toy.
I'll ride it out, I'll keep it bright,
Tomorrow's boat is up in flight!

The Canvas of Unknown Colors

With colors spread across the floor,
I dip my brush, then paint the door.
Is blue for me, or am I red?
Who knew my palette had a thread?

I swipe some green; it looks like grass,
But who on earth would want to pass?
A splash of yellow, oh what fun,
I made a mess—'twas not well done!

The canvas weeps, it looks a fright,
Yet in its chaos, sparks delight.
I laugh at all my clumsy strokes,
The art of life's just a bunch of jokes.

A handprint here, a frown turned smile,
This abstract thing, it takes a while.
But in the mess, there's beauty found,
In every splash, a giggle sound!

Reflections in a Broken Mirror

I gaze at shards that twist and tease,
My face distorted, just like cheese.
Am I a gourmet, or just a snack?
Who knew self-love would cut no slack?

Each piece shows me a brand new face,
I find it funny, this broken space.
I laugh with glee at what I see,
Who needs perfection? Not me!

The mirror cracks, it gives a wink,
Maybe I'll just let it sink.
What's wrong with dancing with a flaw?
In every chip, there's laughter's law.

So here I stand, a jumbled sight,
Yet somehow, it feels just right.
My broken truth, a pure delight,
I celebrate in mirror's light!

Over the Edge of the Familiar

I wake each day with a confused sigh,
Wondering what to eat, oh my, oh my!
Should I have toast or pancakes too?
Decisions, dilemmas, who knew?

I juggle dreams like a circus clown,
Lost and found, yet upside down.
Maybe I'll dance, or just sit tight,
Or wear my socks on the outside, just for spite.

The coffee brews; time slips away,
I think of my goals? Who's to say?
Perhaps I'll open a zoo of cats,
Or write a book on funny hats.

I ponder paths like an old wilted leaf,
Searching for meaning, but finding grief.
Yet laughter bubbles up from within,
Embracing the chaos, I grin again.

Ripples on the Surface

I tossed a coin in the fountain today,
It splashed back, as if to say,
'What do you want? A wish or two?'
I paused and thought, 'I haven't a clue.'

The ducks quacked loudly, they seemed to know,
They planned their day with quite the show.
'Let's swim in circles,' said one with flair,
While I'm stuck here, pulling at my hair.

The sun sparkled like a disco ball,
While I weighed my options, big and small.
Should I bake cookies or fly a kite?
All this pondering feels a bit trite.

So I'll skip the thinking and join the ducks,
Together we'll waddle, avoiding bad luck.
With each silly splash, my worries fade,
In the pond of giggles, I make my parade.

The Garden of Hypothesis

In a garden filled with yellow and blue,
I planted ideas, but none really grew.
Tomatoes of thoughts, they rotted away,
Leaving me baffled at the end of the day.

I tried to sow seeds of grand ambition,
But weeds of distraction plagued my condition.
Though tiny sprouts peeked through the dirt,
Most just chuckled, saying, 'You won't convert.'

The sun shined bright with a golden grin,
As I debated if this was just a spin.
Should I garden more or take a nap?
Maybe write a novel or find a new map?

So I wander through rows of what could be,
Hoping the flowers are kind to me.
With every stumble and silly dance,
I'll learn to relish these random chance.

Essays of the Unknown

I sat down to write a grand ol' tale,
But all that emerged was a floppy snail.
With pens and papers scattered all o'er,
My thoughts played hide and seek, what a chore!

I jotted down dreams, but they took a flight,
I chased them around into the night.
Perhaps I'll pen a guide on how not to care,
Or sketch out a blueprint for dancing bears.

The clock keeps ticking, loud as can be,
Each tick a reminder there's no clear decree.
Shall I list my hopes like a shopping spree?
Or chronicle the times I spilled my tea?

So here I sit, writing what I can,
Hoping for wisdom—perhaps more of a plan.
If nothing else, these essays bring some glee,
As I laugh at the nonsense that's truly just me.

The Quest for the Unseen

I set off on a quest today,
With a map that leads astray.
The treasure is a snack or two,
But no great wisdom in my view.

A squirrel stole my sandwich quick,
Am I searching for a cosmic trick?
The compass spins, oh what a fuss,
Maybe I'll just ride the bus!

I asked a cat for life advice,
She blinked and looked so nice.
Her wisdom? Just a simple yawn,
As I pondered till the dawn.

With every turn I seem to roam,
I realize I forgot my phone.
Still seeking answers, full of cheer,
Next time, I'll just stay right here!

A Soul's Expedition

My soul's on an expedition,
With snacks packed for ingestion.
A guide who's just my reflection,
I'm lost in deep introspection.

Each thought I have is quite absurd,
Like searching for the singing bird.
I found a rock, it looked like gold,
But really, it was just quite old.

In the mirror, I seek the truth,
It's really just my inner youth.
With every step, I trip and fall,
Who knew soul-searching had no protocol?

If wisdom comes with age, they say,
I must be quite the child today.
So I'll keep wandering night and noon,
Chasing answers 'round the moon!

The Road to Discovery

I took the road less traveled by,
But got stuck behind a guy.
His GPS was faulty, too,
Said to follow the painted blue!

Around the bend, I lost my shoe,
Oh dear, now what to do?
The sign says 'wisdom' twenty miles,
But it's hidden behind all these piles!

There's traffic on the route to zen,
Must I wait 'til it's ten again?
The path is winding, leads to snacks,
Or to profound—who needs the facts?

So here I stand, with a grin so wide,
Laughing as I take this ride.
For wisdom's just a funny game,
I think I'll play it just the same!

Fables of Nowhere

In a land where questions reign,
A carrot danced, driving me insane.
It twirled and spun with such delight,
I forgot what I was seeking that night.

There's wisdom in the air whispers low,
But it smells a bit like yesterday's dough.
I followed a duck who quacked so clear,
It led me 'round in circles dear!

The fables told of kings and queens,
Yet here I am with unruly beans.
Every tale a riddle and twist,
Did I find purpose? It's hard to list!

So gather 'round, let's share a laugh,
As we meander on this funny path.
For every quest just might mislead,
Yet humor sure fulfills the need!

The Stillness of Inquiry

In a world of endless choices,
I ponder where to steer my voice.
With each step taken, I pause and grin,
Is this the time to dive right in?

Cookies or cakes, the dilemma grows,
With every flavor, my purpose slows.
Questions whirl like leaves in fall,
Am I meant to lead, or just to crawl?

Each day I ponder, laugh, and sigh,
Do fishes dream, or just swim by?
The answers hide by the fridge's door,
Maybe pickles are what I'm looking for?

In the stillness, I tap my chin,
More naps and snacks, where to begin?
Lighthearted thoughts, like balloons in sky,
Should I chase my dreams, or just eat pie?

Beyond the Horizon

I squint at horizons, bright and wide,
Thinking of journeys, full of pride.
Where's this path taking me today?
Is that a detour, or just a buffet?

Maps all seem to point in a mess,
I ask for help, they just confess.
Follow the road! They all shout loud,
But I prefer the comfort of a crowd.

Adventure calls, but my couch looks nice,
Shiny new moments or yesterday's rice?
Do I need a quest or just more tea?
Maybe wisdom's hiding in snacks, you see.

Beyond the horizon, dreams are vast,
Yet Netflix reminds me of the past.
With popcorn ready, what will I choose?
A life of questions, but no time to lose!

The Heart's Enigma

My heart is a riddle, a tricky maze,
Full of thoughts that set me ablaze.
With each laugh from a friend so dear,
I wonder if joy's the goal right here?

Sometimes it's simple, like wearing socks,
Or dancing wildly, oh what a paradox!
With every beat, a question grows,
Is my true self lost in the shows?

I search for meaning in cookie crumbs,
In laughter and jokes, in silly drums.
Why so serious, that's so passé,
Let's find our way in a fun ballet!

The enigma of hearts might never fade,
It dances along in a playful parade.
With each conundrum, I'll raise a cheer,
For all my doubts, I'll embrace the queer!

Breathing in Questions

Inhale the wonder, exhale the doubt,
What's it all for? I'm missing out!
Between each breath, a giggle stirs,
Are we just dolls, or do we have spurs?

Counting the stars, or just the snacks?
Here's to finding balance, but where are my racks?
Do jellybeans hold the answers I seek?
Or is wisdom found in my comfy sneaks?

Searching for meaning like a cat in a box,
Should I think hard or just relax?
Every question feels light as a breeze,
Should I dance, or simply sneeze?

Breathing in questions brings a big smile,
As I ponder this path, with a little style.
Each laugh leads me further in,
What's the key? To simply begin!

Footsteps in the Mist

I woke up one day, where to go?
The cereal box said, but it was slow.
My GPS blinked, 'Turn left or right?'
I ended up lost, but oh what a sight!

With a coffee in hand, I strolled around,
Chasing my thoughts on haphazard ground.
A cat crossed my path, with a wise old stare,
I wondered if he planned his own lair.

Each step I take feels like a jest,
As I ponder my goals with a whimsical quest.
A rollercoaster of twists, highs, and lows,
Maybe I'll find it out wearing a nose!

But with laughter beside me and joy in my heart,
Maybe the answer was just making art.
So I'll scribble my dreams, let the nonsense flow,
Tomorrow's a puzzle, let's see what it shows.

In Pursuit of Tomorrow

With a coffee mug held high, I start my day,
To conquer the world in a very lost way.
Chasing the sun like a moth to a flame,
But end up in circles, I'm always the same.

A job in my thoughts, or maybe a band?
Do I write my memoirs or sit on the sand?
The clock hands tick-tock, setting pace to the race,
Each idea I ponder just adds to the chase.

The calendar laughs, it's all just a game,
I thought I had purpose, but none is the same.
I'll dance with the doubts while I shimmy and sway,
Finding my fortune in a humorous way.

So here's to tomorrow, wherever it hides,
With a wink and a grin, let humor be my guide.
I'll twirl through the week like a clown in a hat,
With joy as my compass, there's no room for flat!

The Puzzle Unfinished

A puzzle of life, with jigsaws galore,
I'm missing some pieces, and maybe a score.
Each time I try to connect the right parts,
I end up with chaos, oh how it imparts!

Found humor in edges, straight lines look great,
But what's with the colors? I'm questioning fate.
I'd trade in my pieces for a map or a sign,
Still, lost in this jumble, all twisted in twine.

Riding on trains that go nowhere fast,
I giggle at choices, my future forecast.
Like socks in the dryer, they disappear fast,
Maybe I'll find them, just not in this class.

But give me a riddle, a laugh, and a friend,
Perhaps all this nonsense leads to a trend.
With each brand-new piece, I'll cherish the chase,
In a puzzle unfinished, I've found my own space.

A Journey Without a Map

I set out one morning, my map all but fake,
With a wink and a nod, I embraced what's at stake.
Adventure awaits, or so I was told,
Yet here I am wandering, feeling quite bold.

The road winds and bends like a noodle in soup,
Each twist and each turn makes me smile at the loop.
I asked for direction, but dogs just would bark,
Turns out they're all masters of a life in the park.

Oh, a previous plan crumpled like old tin foil,
But laughter is better than itching to toil.
I'll pick fruit while dancing to tunes on the breeze,
Who needs a grand strategy when life's such a tease?

So here's to the journey, no limits in sight,
With joy in my heart, every mistake feels just right.
A route that's uncharted? I'm ready to roam!
For those yet to come, I'll just bring them along!

Moments of Reflection

I ponder deeply, what's the plan?
A map unfolded, lost in the span.
Coffee in hand, I sit and muse,
Is it pizza or dreams I should choose?

The clock keeps ticking, a relentless tick,
Is that my fate or just a trick?
I tried to fly but fell like a lump,
Just a toaster, I can't even jump.

With all these thoughts, I start to think,
Am I a pen or just the ink?
Wading through puddles of dreams unmet,
I laugh and sigh, can't find the jet.

So here I am, sipping my tea,
Where's the goal? Who's the real me?
In this circus act, I lose my place,
But life's a joke, and I wear the face.

The Labyrinth of Existence

In a maze of choices, I roam each day,
Do I want broccoli, or just some hay?
A fork in the road, one path is bright,
The other looks more like a good night fight.

I'm chasing stars in a paper bag,
Maybe I'm just a tired old rag.
Finding my way with a cardboard map,
Still walking in circles, perhaps a nap?

Is it the cheese or the trap I seek?
Everywhere I turn, I feel so bleak.
With laughter echoing, I take a step,
Back to my couch for a comfy pep.

In this grand maze, I lose my grind,
Yet every twist feels jumbled and blind.
I find my joy in the silliest ways,
Perhaps I'll just dance in a crazy craze.

Echoes of the Heart

I shout my dreams into the void,
Hoping they stick like old gum, annoyed.
Echoes bounce back, a holler of glee,
But was that my heart, or just a bee?

With each attempt, I find a snare,
Is it ambition or just hot air?
Stumbling through hopes like a wobbly fool,
I laugh at the chaos, that's my rule.

The heart keeps beating, oh so loud,
Making strange sounds, like a strange crowd.
I gather the echoes, put them in jars,
Plan to release them beneath the stars.

So here's my heart, a clown with a smile,
A jester in dreams, it's been a while.
Life's a riddle wrapped in a wink,
And I'll keep dancing, as I think.

The Symphony of Uncertainty

In the orchestra of life, I pluck my strings,
Playing notes that do funny things.
A dash of confusion, a sprinkle of cheer,
Why is my conductor never near?

Like a tambourine, I shake without care,
Lost in the rhythm, do I even dare?
My notes clash wildly, a cacophony loud,
But somehow I shine, feel oddly proud.

In a world of harmony, chaos does dwell,
I ask myself, is this heaven or hell?
I dance on the beats that don't fit the score,
And laugh at the mess that I can't ignore.

So here's my tale, a symphony rare,
With each awkward beat, I find my flair.
In the laughter and chaos, I find my art,
A funny little life, straight from the heart.

Whispers of the Undecided

In the mirror, I stare, wondering why,
Should I bake or should I just fly?
Coffee in hand, socks mismatched,
To find my call, I feel detached.

Should I knit or should I dance?
In this grand life, I've taken a chance.
With choices like cereal or toast,
I'll figure it out; I'm not too engrossed.

A sandwich or causing a fuss?
Flip a coin; it's all a big plus.
Birds sing sweet, but I can't find,
If dreams are near or left behind.

I'll take a stroll, just me and my shoes,
In a world of options, I can't lose.
Perhaps a taco calls my name,
To decide is tough; it's all a game.

Searching for Stars in Daylight

Staring at clouds, what a fine show,
Those donkeys in dreams, or just cotton fluff? Who knows?
Chasing bright thoughts that slip away,
Like my sock when I just wanna play.

The sun is up; where are the stars?
Do they hide behind the town's far bars?
I ask my cat; he just yawns wide,
He's gotten comfy, so I must abide.

Should I jump the fence or stay here and snore?
Might as well stay in with some chips on the floor.
Coffee on the side, a grin on my face,
In a world so bright, I'm lost in the race.

Now let's ponder on what this means,
Can hotdogs sing? Or is that just dreams?
Maybe tomorrow will bring some fun,
And I'll figure out what I've truly begun.

The Map with No Destination

I've got a map with doodles and lines,
Maybe to Paris or just some pines?
Flip it upside down, what will I see?
Perhaps a pizza shop calling to me!

Directionless, like socks in the dryer,
Each page is a trail, each squiggle, a flyer.
Should I turn left or dash to the right?
Oh look! A bird! Let's follow its flight.

"Adventure awaits!" they all like to say,
I'm still confused about what's in my way.
Should I travel by car or by bike?
Or simply to walk with my trusty old pike?

My heart beats fast, but am I awake?
Straying from maps, that's all it will take.
To find where I'm going, I'll just need some cheer,
Maybe brunch with my pals will soon make it clear.

Paths Unwalked and Roads Unseen

I see paths unwalked, waiting for me,
Would it be smart to climb that big tree?
With friends all giggling at every twist,
Who knew being lost could feel like bliss?

Through the brambles, I chase a thought,
What was it that I really sought?
Perhaps a nap, or just more snacks,
Let's roam around until the clock cracks.

Piggyback rides or running amok,
Maybe a quest to catch a lucky rock?
Life's little puzzles twist my head,
But laughter with pals brings joy instead.

So here's to roads that flutter and sway,
To muddled moments that lead us to play.
With wonder, I wander, feel light as a feather,
And giggle at choices that just don't matter.

Notes from an Unwritten Journey

On the map of dreams, I doodle and scribble,
A treasure chest marked with a question, a riddle.
With every wrong turn, I smile and I laugh,
Mixing a cocktail of fate and a gaffe.

I trip on the path, but it dances with glee,
A sassy little sprite that just won't let me be.
I juggle my thoughts, like a clown at a fair,
Is it wisdom I seek, or just more silly air?

A fork in the road, one leads to a snack,
The other a journey, endless and black.
Do I follow my stomach or heed the old sage?
Maybe I'll flip a coin, I'm not yet of age.

So here I stand, lost amid all the cheer,
With sarcasm as my guide, I stumble sincere.
Tracking the nonsense in my curious quest,
Who says life isn't fun when you just jest?

The Silent Symphony of Choices

In a world full of options, I'm here with my soup,
Should I add in some spice or just join the loop?
Every choice feels masterful, like basic ballet,
Yet I end up twirling in a confused array.

The pizza slice whispers, 'Pick me, eat first!'
But the salad yells louder, a vegetable burst.
I'm stuck in this concert, my stomach in tow,
In the symphonic chaos, what's next? I don't know!

Oh look, it's a donut, a sugary foe,
With sprinkles and magic, it steals the show.
I dance with my cravings, so wild and free,
While pondering deep questions: Who's smarter, me or my belly?

With a wink to the moon, I take a deep breath,
Choices bounce around, life's quirky pest.
This silent symphony plays for one only,
As I sing off-key, never sad, just a phony.

Fleeting Shadows of Tomorrow

Tomorrow looms close, like a cat up a tree,
Will I slide down gently, or fall with a spree?
I wave at the future, but it giggles away,
Like a prankster in time, just wanting to play.

Today feels like ice cream, a scoop of delight,
But tomorrow's like broccoli—yikes! What a fright!
I hold out my spoon, with a frown and a laugh,
Will I savor the sweetness or gobble the chaff?

Chasing shadows in sunlight, I trip on my feet,
With each silly step, I taste life's little treat.
Laughter echoes softly, while my worries just run,
Is the best part of living the journey or fun?

So here's to the missteps, the giggles and sighs,
With toppings of chaos like bright summer skies.
In the fleeting of moments, I ponder and roam,
Maybe the shadow is where I find home.

The Elegy of a Hesitant Heart

Oh dear, what's this mess? A heart turning slow,
It tiptoes in circles, unsure where to go.
With a trumpet half-blown, it stammers a tune,
Like a cat on a fence under the light of the moon.

I'm torn between sunshine and dark, rainy nights,
Should I wear yellow socks or embrace all my fights?
The heart makes decisions like flipping a coin,
But which side is wise? I cannot rejoin.

It flutters like butterflies caught in a storm,
With indecision wrapped up in a cozy warm form.
Oh, what a lovely dance—will it ever expect?
With two left feet, it just dodges respect.

But laughter erupts, and I chuckle inside,
For my hesitant heart takes a silly ride.
In the elegy sung, there's joy in the blend,
For life's little tangles give reason to mend.

Tangled Threads of Thought

In a maze of socks I tread,
Wandering thoughts, a tangle spread.
Where's my coffee, where's my phone?
I trip on dreams like old, lost bone.

Chasing tails of grand designs,
Yet I can't recall the signs.
Life's a puzzle with a twist,
Should I scream or just resist?

Mind's a cat with nine lives to spare,
Pouncing on doubt like it's a dare.
Every moment, a playful tease,
Like a sneeze that comes with cheese.

With a chuckle, I miss the mark,
Like a candle in a park.
But oh, these threads, they weave and swirl,
In my chaotic, joyful whirl.

An Unwritten Script

I wander on a stage of fate,
My lines seem late, no worries, mate.
The spotlight flickers with confusion,
Where's the plot in this illusion?

A director with a faulty cue,
Tosses scripts like yesterday's stew.
I stand here, props in hand, so grand,
Saying, "Who wrote this? Not I, man!"

Every act a comedy of errors,
Fumbling lines from eager terrors.
The audience cracks up with glee,
As I forget to take a pee!

So let the curtains rise and fall,
I'll juggle acts, I'll chance it all.
For in this chaos, I find my groove,
Dancing to tunes that always move.

Stardust Dreams

I dream in colors bright and wide,
A galaxy where silliness hides.
Comets dance like party clowns,
While I float in my fuzzy gowns.

Stars whisper secrets, oh so sly,
"Should you twirl or just comply?"
I spin around like a merry go,
In the glitter where the pixies flow.

Picking wishes, a cosmic trade,
Buying time with lemonade.
But when I sip, the cup is cracked,
And all my plans remain unpacked.

Yet laughter echoes through the spheres,
With every giggle, melt my fears.
Stardust dreams may miss the mark,
But oh, how bright they shine in dark!

Flickers of Resolve

I light a candle, then I sigh,
What was the goal? Oh me, oh my!
Flames dance wildly, a funny jest,
As I ponder where I'll rest.

Armed with coffee and a grin,
I chase my shadow that wore thin.
Oh, sweet indecision, come sit down,
We'll plot together, silly frown.

In this blip called the everyday,
I toss my plans like autumn play.
With every stumble, with every fall,
Flickers of hope seem short and small.

But here's the joke in this charade,
We find the light when plans do fade.
So let's giggle at the turns we take,
In the jigsaw puzzle, it's laugh or break!

Echoes of Uncertainty

I wake up each morning, yes, it's true,
But what am I doing? No clue, oh boo.
I've mapped out my goals, they all seem bright,
Yet I stumble and fumble from morning to night.

In coffee I trust, my caffeinated card,
Yet dreams still feel distant, and thoughts come hard.
Do I chase after rainbows or stay in my lane?
I laugh at the chaos, it drives me insane.

The universe whispers, or maybe it shouts,
But my head's in a whirlpool of curious doubts.
Perhaps I'll be wise, on an old rocking chair,
While wondering how I ended up here without care.

So here I am bouncing, like a ball in a game,
Trying to figure out, who's really to blame.
But hey, what's the rush? Let's laugh at the ride,
In this circus of questions, I'll chuckle with pride.

Threads of a Wandering Mind

Thoughts flit like butterflies, never stay still,
I chase them around, what a crazy thrill!
I scribble my dreams on the back of my hand,
But forget all their colors, they're hard to understand.

I wander through forests of 'what if' and 'who knows',
Tripping on visions where confusion just grows.
Should I follow the squirrels or take to the skies?
The map says 'go right', but I can't read the signs.

My friends say 'grow up', but I giggle and tease,
I'm too busy pondering the life of a bee.
With honey as wisdom, and flowers as fate,
I'm lost in the humor of figuring great!

In the circus of musings, I take my front seat,
The laughter of chance makes my journey complete.
So here's to the chaos, the joy in the mess,
With threads on the floor, I'll just call it progress.

The Puzzle with Missing Pieces

A jigsaw of dreams, but I'm missing a part,
Try fitting in hopes, but they don't seem too smart.
I scour through my box, what a colorful crash,
But the corner pieces vanish, oh what a splash!

I tried to assemble the stories I'd weave,
Yet half of the picture's just hard to believe.
Do I have the edge pieces, or is this just fun?
I laugh at the chaos, it's never quite done.

Every time that I think I am ready to frame,
Another loose bit seems to mess with my aim.
With laughter, I toss them—oh what a delight,
It's like a wild party each puzzling night!

So I'll raise a toast to the gaps and the holes,
To the funny misfits, the lost little souls.
Here's to the nonsense, the madness to tame,
In this game of confusion, I've staked my claim!

Dreams Adrift on Distant Shores

I set sail with visions, they wave from afar,
But the compass is broken, oh what a bizarre!
Are those dreams just mirages, illusions in stride?
Or crabs in the sand that I cannot abide?

The waves toss my thoughts, oh how they do dance,
I'm looking for answers, but where's my chance?
Each ripple a question, each splash gets me bold,
But the beach ball of purpose, it won't be controlled.

With treasures of laughter, I dig in the sand,
But the map's in a riddle, it slips from my hand.
I'll find that odd shell, or perhaps a lost shoe,
And wonder if fortune is playing a view.

So let's float on our dreams, on this cosmic bay,
With fins of confusion, we'll simply sway.
In the sea of uncertainty, where joy often pours,
I'll surf on the waves, as adventure explores.

Chasing Echoes of a Faint Tomorrow

I woke up today and forgot my goal,
My coffee's cold, I'm stuck in a hole.
The birds are chirping, but I hear no song,
Maybe I should just tag along.

The cat's on the counter, quite the debate,
While I ponder how to captivate fate.
A missed opportunity turned into a dance,
Guess I'll just wait for a second chance.

Pursuing shadows in a grocery line,
Where's my cart? It's time to opine.
I thought about saving, but then I just shopped,
Now my bank account's become quite the flop.

Tomorrow is fleeting, like socks mismatched,
Chasing my echo, I seem quite detached.
Faint hopes are dancing, making me grin,
Who knew confusion could feel like a win?

In Search of the Unfindable

I set off this morning, adventure in mind,
With a map of nothing, I hope to find.
The treasure I seek seems lost in my head,
Maybe I'll find it under my bed.

I asked a wise owl, but he hooted and fled,
Claimed he was busy, which filled me with dread.
I followed a squirrel; he led me astray,
Now I'm stuck wondering if I should stay.

The universe chuckles, as I trip on a stone,
Riding the waves of the great unknown.
What's worth discovering? An unsolved riddle,
I guess I'll keep playing this strange fiddle.

Is happiness lost, or just misplaced?
I'll search high and low, with grace and some haste.
Inquiries galore, yet answers are few,
Guess I'll just waffle, that's what I'll do!

The Shadow of a Dream Half-Formed

I had a sweet dream, but it flitted away,
Like ice cream melting on a sunny day.
Half-formed ideas float like balloons,
While I chase them around, singing silly tunes.

The shadow of ambition lurks in the back,
Hiding from sunlight, keeping on track.
I ponder its meaning as I twirl in my chair,
Does anyone know if I'm getting somewhere?

The clock is tick-tocking, what's the plan today?
I'll write down my dreams and then misplace the page.
Ideas like butterflies, they flicker and flap,
Awkwardly waltzing through this oversized map.

I try to connect the dots that don't meet,
In a jigsaw puzzle, now that's quite a feat!
Finding the shadow seems slightly absurd,
Yet here I am, laughing, slightly perturbed.

Navigating Through the Gloom

Wandering aimlessly, I trip on a shoelace,
In this gloomy maze, can't find my place.
A cloud of confusion hangs over my head,
Looking for answers while just eating bread.

The sun sometimes peeks, but I squint and groan,
In this fog of indecision, I feel all alone.
I asked a wise sage, but he just ate fries,
Guess wisdom's on hold as it munches and sighs.

Navigating tangled thoughts, left and right,
Stumbled upon hope, then it took flight.
Is that a light at the end, or a train?
With humor intact, this feels like a game.

So here's to the journey and its twisty turns,
May we laugh at the chaos while the wisdom churns.
In this nonsensical dance, we can find our groove,
Even when feeling a tad out of move!

Dances with Destiny

I twirl to the left, then step to the right,
My future looks hazy, but feels so polite.
Do I dance with the stars or slide on a shoe?
Perhaps it's a tango with someone like you.

Should I cha-cha with fate or simply moonwalk?
Should I leap through the air or just sit here and talk?
With every misstep, I chuckle and grin,
Who knew the waltz could be such a win?

Unveiling the Veil

A crystal ball glimmers, yet shows me a cat,
The secrets of life draped in this silly hat.
I lift up the veil, find a peanut instead,
A snack for a journey, what lies up ahead?

In search of truth, I ask silly old trees,
They just sway and whisper, beg me to sneeze.
With branches of wisdom and roots full of jest,
I giggle and nod, but still feel like a guest.

The Art of Wandering

I roam through the streets, no map in my hand,
Each corner I turn brings a new rubber band.
A compass is nice, but I'd rather lose track,
Exploring the snacks that will fill up my sack.

The clock strikes a tune, I dance with a breeze,
Lost in the shuffle, oh, what fun it frees!
Who needs a destination or reason to roam?
Each step is a puzzle, each twist is a poem.

Crossroads of Confusion

I stand at a junction, unsure where to go,
Left leads to bakery, while right says, 'Hello!'
A signpost is baffled, it points just like me,
How to ponder purpose while munching on brie?

Do I take the detour or follow the bliss?
Every option looks tempting, how can I miss?
A rabbit in a top hat says, 'Join in the fun!'
With laughter as my guide, I'll chase until done.

Melodies of an Uncertain Tune

I woke up today, chose socks that don't match,
Thought I'd find wisdom in my morning batch.
Coffee in hand, heart full of cheer,
But the toaster just burned my breakfast, oh dear!

A cat on my lap, he seems so wise,
Yet all he does is nap and rise.
I ask him my fate, he just yawns away,
Maybe he knows the secrets, but he won't say.

The mirror reflects a face full of doubt,
Where have all my bright dreams gone out?
I hum a tune, it's slightly off-key,
But maybe that's just the sound of me!

So I dance to this rhythm, a little absurd,
Twist and twirl, just to be heard.
With laughter in heart and a wiggle in my step,
I might just stumble on joy, as I misstep!

A Tapestry Woven with Questions

Threads of thoughts, tangled and wild,
Picture me lost, like a confused child.
Stitching my dreams on a fraying seam,
Wondering sometimes, if I'm just a meme!

Why is that old man, so wise and spry,
Wearing socks with sandals, I can't deny?
His giggles echo with wisdom untold,
Maybe he knows, and he's just being bold.

I ponder the stars from my rickety chair,
Finding meaning in dust, floating in air.
Some days a genius, some days a fool,
Might be a sign that I skipped school!

A tapestry grand, yet so full of holes,
With patches of laughter and odd little roles.
With each stitch I take, may I twine and weave,
A pattern of giggles, and that's what I believe!

Searching for Meaning

I peep through the window, what do I see?
A squirrel on a mission, is it just looking for cheese?
I laugh at the critter, all frantic and scurry,
   Am I just like him, in such a hurry?

My boss always says, 'Find that great role,'
But half the time, I can't even find my soul.
I check behind couches, inside my shoe,
   It seems my existence is quite askew!

With a map in my hand, I'm lost at sea,
A compass that spins, what could it be?
They say seek and you will find the prize,
   But I found some socks and a bunch of lies!

So I chuckle and shrug, with a wink and a grin,
Perhaps the real treasure was always within.
In the quest for the truth, the laughter I glean,
   Is the happiest meaning I've ever seen!

The Uncharted Path

On this uncharted path, my GPS died,
So I follow the birds, let them be my guide.
Their chatter is nonsensical, much like my head,
As I trip over roots, my confidence fled!

Do I turn left to wisdom, or right for a jest?
Each choice is a riddle, a quirky test.
Jumping over puddles, I slip and I slide,
Is this what they meant by the adventurous ride?

Oh, the trees talk to me, in whispers and sighs,
Spilling their secrets under cloudy skies.
I squint at the trail, is that wisdom I see?
Or just a dog chasing shadows, mocking me?

At the end of each journey, I find my own way,
Chuckling at missteps that led me to play.
With each twist and turn, maybe I'm blessed,
In this silly dance of an uncharted quest!

Twilight of Doubt

In the twilight where shadows play,
I ponder my choices, what a display!
Should I dance or take a nap?
Oh, where's the fun in a boring map?

Socks mismatched, I'm on my way,
To find the answers by the end of the day.
Waffles or pancakes? Oh, what a fight!
Not sure about purpose, but I'll have a bite!

A Tapestry of Choices

Threads of laughter weave my day,
Each choice a stitch in a quirky way.
Do I flip the coin or toss a shoe?
Either way, I'll end up in a stew!

The fabric's frayed but it's all fun,
Stitching my dreams in the blazing sun.
Career paths tangled in a wild dance,
Should I sing, or bake, or take a chance?

The Journey Within

I set out to seek inner peace,
But found my socks and that's a tease.
Meditation, a calming place,
Unless the cat decides to race!

Questions swirl like leaves in fall,
I ask myself, "Is this all?"
With every turn, I trip and spin,
But hey, at least I'm learning to grin!

Seeds of Possibility

I planted dreams in a garden of doubt,
Watered with giggles, but there's a rout.
Some bloomed flowers, some turned to weeds,
Still, I dance around, ignoring the creeds.

Sunshine or rain? Who knows today?
With every turn, I just want to play.
The more I dig, the more I find,
The seeds of laughter grow in my mind!

The Question of What Lies Ahead

What's next on this wild ride?
Lost in a fog, I just slide.
Should I be a painter, or baker?
Maybe a couch potato, for the fun maker?

I whisper to the stars at night,
They respond with cosmic fright.
A fortune cookie said, 'Just relax!',
But I'm here with my mind full of cracks.

The coffee shop buzzes, I sip my brew,
Contemplating all the things I could do.
Back to doodling fortunes on a napkin,
Scribbling hopes in a wayward fashion.

It's a circus act, no doubt about that,
With a juggling act of a cat and a hat.
One day a hero, the next a goat,
Taking leaps on this tightrope of hope.

Dancing with Doubt

Two left feet on this dance floor,
Wobbling like I'm closing a door.
Should I shuffle right or twist to the left?
The rhythm of life is feeling like theft.

With sunglasses on, I strut about,
But inside, I'm just filled with doubt.
A waltz with concerns, all dressed up in fear,
Do I dare to take the next step near?

The DJ spins tunes of dreams hard to find,
With every spin, my head gets unlined.
I laughed so loud, I nearly fell,
On this dance floor of "What the heck!" well.

But maybe I'll twirl, just one more time,
To dizzy away this mountain to climb.
After all, who says it must make sense?
Letting go can be such a suspense.

A Compass without North

My compass spins in wild delight,
With no true direction in sight.
Do I follow where the wind may blow,
Or stay put and watch the grass grow?

They say 'find your way,' but where is that?
I'm chasing my tail like a confused cat.
If life's a journey, I misplaced the map,
Now I'm tripping in this epic mishap.

Mapquest says turn left, I'll try the right,
I'll stumble on until I feel just right.
At least the detours lead to good snacks,
Who knew lost could come with a few laughs?

So here I wander, no path to trace,
Just a smile on my confused face.
With no compass to guide, I'm feeling free,
Who knows where this wacky ride will lead me?

Fragmented Aspirations

A dream of being a rockstar once bloomed,
Now I'm just here, stuck in my room.
Instead of a stage, I sing in the shower,
With shampoo as my crowd of power.

At breakfast, I wish for a career worth noting,
Sipping my cereal while my plans go floating.
Should I write a novel or bake a fine cake?
Guess I'll just flip through Netflix for a break.

With sticky notes cluttering my space,
My future's a clutter, a chaotic place.
But each time I step into shoes of the bold,
I realize, it's all just a story untold.

So here's to the scrap and the cluttered plans,
Dancing in circles, constructing strands.
With laughs as my compass, I'll wander a bit,
In this weird game, I will never quite quit.

Beneath the Surface

I woke up today, tried to find my way,
A coffee in hand, hopes gone astray.
Should I chase a dream or take a nap?
The cat just laughed, curled in my lap.

Thoughts swirl like soup, thick and unclear,
What do I want? Or is it a beer?
I could climb a mountain or binge a show,
But that seems too hard; oh where do I go?

Life's like a puzzle, missing a piece,
I tried to fit in, but got no release.
The puzzle box promised a grand design,
But all I found was a random line.

They say to be brave, take life by storm,
But I tripped on my shoelace; is that the norm?
With every new choice, I just feel more lost,
Should I flip a coin, no matter the cost?

The Weight of Wonder

They say to keep asking, what am I for?
I asked my goldfish, he swam to the shore.
My lunch tried to tell me, but I just ate,
Got lost in my sandwich, what a twist of fate!

Juggling my wishes like balls in the air,
One slipped and shattered, did I even care?
A job, a kid, a house on the hill,
But I still can't figure out how to chill.

They sell you a dream wrapped up in a bow,
But what do you do when that bow won't go?
I asked my dog, he just chased his tail,
Was he on to something, or just off the trail?

So here I am, smiling under the weight,
Of questions unending, but hey, that's fate.
I'll keep on dancing, with life as my song,
In a waltz of confusion, where's the right wrong?

Roads Less Traveled

Hit the fork in the road, which way to pick?
Left leads to work, right to a picnic.
The squirrels are judging, with acorn disdain,
Should I buckle down or dance in the rain?

Maps promise clarity, but they seem a tease,
Like my GPS, always lost in the trees.
I'll caravan with strangers, or maybe just me,
A road trip to nowhere sounds nice as can be.

Life's a buffet, but I'm stuck on pie,
Adventurous salads just make me sigh.
Every step is a question, each mile an unsung,
But wait—what's that smell? Oh look! A bun.

So off I go, laughing through every bend,
A wonderer's heart, it will never end.
If I can't find the answers, I'll just make a friend,
At the edge of confusion, my soul will ascend!

The Fickle Flame

I lit a candle, thought I'd find some cheer,
But it flickered out, and then disappeared.
Like motivation on a Monday so dreary,
Or a shoe that unlaces when things get too cheery.

Thought I'd blaze paths with a passionate spark,
But my plans burned out, igniting the dark.
Maybe I'll camp and toast marshmallow dreams,
Instead of chasing life's slippery schemes.

So here's a bright notion: let's bubble and boil,
Turn worries to giggles, let joy be our soil.
The flame of confusion can warm up the night,
At least I can roast my uncertainty right.

So raise a toast to our whimsical fate,
We'll laugh at the flame, it's never too late.
With each little flicker, we'll find silly fun,
In the glow of our chaos, let's shine as one!

Beneath the Stars

Under the sky, I ponder and sigh,
Waiting for answers, oh my, oh my!
The stars just twinkle, with no clear direction,
Maybe they're just playing, a cosmic collection.

I asked a wise owl, all stout on a limb,
"What's the point, dear friend?", I asked on a whim.
He hooted and chuckled, then flew off in a blur,
Leaving me thinking, was that really a cure?

I tried a fortune cookie, it crunched with delight,
"Your future is fuzzy, but the soup's just right!"
So here I am wondering, with noodles in hand,
Is it all just a joke, or some grand, silly plan?

Underneath all the laughter, the mischief and fun,
I search for a sign, a riddle to be spun.
Maybe the secret's, to dance with the breeze,
And embrace every question, just like a tease.

The Dance of Paradox

In the carousel of life, round and round,
Answers escape like balloons unbound.
One moment I'm serious, the next I'm a fool,
Waltzing in circles, breaking every rule.

A jester once told me, "Look for the laugh!",
But I just keep spiraling, lost in the bath.
Is it depth I seek, or just a rubber duck?
The universe chuckles, it's a comedy truck!

I ponder the meaning over pie à la mode,
Scribbling my thoughts on a candy-cane road.
Do stars know their purpose while twinkling away?
Or do they just shimmer, then fade to gray?

Feathers and contradictions, they dance in a line,
Twirling between reason and silly design.
I'll join in the folly, with giggles and cheer,
Embracing the chaos, no reason to fear!

Weathering the Storm

Raindrops are falling, my hair's a big mess,
Life's throwing curveballs, I must reassess.
Coffee's a lifeline, my friend in distress,
Is it too much to ask for a bit of finesse?

I built a fort made of blankets and sheets,
Hiding from chaos, the drama it greets.
Inside, I sip cocoa, wrapped up like a taco,
Wondering if thunder is just nature's bravado.

The wind howls like demons, but I chuckle back loud,
I'm laughing at clouds while feeling all proud.
My life's a tornado, a whimsical swirl,
With giggles and fumbles, it makes my head twirl!

When sunshine peeks in, I give a sly wink,
For every odd moment, there's room to rethink.
So bring on the storm, I'm ready for glee,
In the heart of the tempest, I dance like I'm free!

The Veiled Horizon

Distant horizons hold secrets untold,
Wrapped in a riddle, shiny like gold.
I squint at the future, it waves from afar,
Like a shy child playing peek-a-boo in a car.

With a map in my pocket, I chase the unknown,
Every turn is a giggle, it feels like a throne.
Is that wisdom or whimsy that leads me today?
Maybe it's just waffles that brighten my way!

I climbed a tall mountain, searching for signs,
Just to find ice-cream shops with funky designs.
The cosmos might giggle, in its cosmic array,
As I trade grand ambitions for sprinkles and play.

So give me the veils, the puns and the jest,
I'm savoring laughter, it's truly the best.
Beyond the horizon, come join in the dance,
For each twist and turn, well, it's all just a chance!

Whispers of Uncertainty

I woke up today with a plan in mind,
But breakfast intervened, oh how unkind!
Should I bake a cake or write a book?
Confusion reigns with every little look.

The universe giggles at my indecisive dance,
Do I take the chance or just leave it to chance?
With every step, I trip on my own feet,
Life's a circus act, and I'm losing my seat.

The GPS says turn but I just drive straight,
Perhaps I'll figure things out on another date.
The map's upside down, what a sight to behold,
Wandering, I find treasures better than gold.

So here I am, a comedy in motion,
With every misguided step, a new ocean.
Uncertainty's funny when we take a glance,
At the quirks of our journey, a spontaneous dance.

Chasing Shadows of Intent

I set off seeking wisdom, my thoughts in a race,
But a squirrel stole my sandwich; what a disgrace!
Should I ponder the cosmos or play with my socks?
Philosophy fails when you've lost your lunch box.

I wrote down my dreams in a haphazard scrawl,
Yet the pen went dry; that's my luck, after all.
Should I chase wisdom or chase after bread?
Maybe both will collide inside my head.

With each clever thought, another one slips,
Like ice on my driveway, it's all just full flips.
Do I want to be serious or just have some fun?
Decisions get heavy like lifting a ton.

In this game of confusion, the score is quite clear,
I laugh at my choices, and drink another beer.
Intentions like shadows just flit in the light,
Dancing away while I ponder all night.

Questions Without Answers

Why do socks vanish? I ponder this plight,
While munching on popcorn, oh what a delight!
Searching for meaning in my morning tea,
But all that I find is a crumb from a spree.

What is our quest? Is it more pizza or pie?
As I glance at my napkin, and let out a sigh.
Should I chase the horizon or stick to my bed?
These questions abound, causing chaos in my head.

If I dance with a penguin, will the world make sense?
Or should I just nap, it's less intense?
When in doubt, I consult with my cat,
But she's busy plotting a sneaky attack.

So here I stand, with questions galore,
Why do doors squeak and what's out of store?
While I muddle through answers that never quite land,
I find peace in confusion; it's perfectly planned.

Navigating the Unknown

I tried to go left but ended up right,
Lost in a maze of snack runs at night.
The map said "detour," but my heart yelled "go!"
Forget the GPS; I'm just here for the show.

In the land of the lost, I found a new plan,
To dance with the weird, become my own fan.
A twist in the road leads to laughter and fun,
Navigating chaos, like donuts on the run.

With questions like candy, all sticky and sweet,
I'll savor each moment and embrace the retreat.
Should I pull on that thread or let it unwind?
The fabric of life is a riot, unkind.

So here in the unknown, I'll twirl and I'll spin,
With laughter as my compass, let the adventure begin!
Who needs a map when the path is a joke?
Just follow the giggles; the fun is bespoke.

Seasons of Inquiry

In spring I plant my grand to-do,
Yet summer's sun just bakes the stew.
Autumn leaves, they whisper doubt,
While winter's chill makes me want out.

Tried to find my calling last fall,
Missed it again, it's a free-for-all.
They say look up, check the stars,
Yet here I am, still munching on bars.

The path is twisted, full of fun,
Trying to figure if it's all a run.
I'll just play along with the jest,
And wear my confusion like a fest.

So here's to the quest, I'll teleport,
To the land of "Why?" and "What's the sport?"
With silly hats and a smirk, I'll take a chance,
Maybe purpose is just a groovy dance!

Fragments of Understanding

Picked up a puzzle, missing some bits,
Held it to the light—oh, what fits?
Thought I found the corner piece,
But it was just a chocolate feast.

Running around in circles, whee!
Grabbing at answers like a bee.
"Do what you love," they all will cheer,
But I like napping and homebrew beer.

Philosophers argue, they're so profound,
While I'm here just spinning around.
Perhaps my calling's to avoid the call,
And hang out with snacks—that's the best ball.

Fragments of thoughts, all jumbled, oh dear!
Mixing my dreams with a pinch of fear.
If humor's a guide on this wacky road,
I'll ride through chaos with my humor bestowed!

A Heart Adrift

My heart's a boat; the sail's in a twist,
Drifting around, like an uninvited guest.
"What's the meaning?" I ask the sky,
But the clouds just laugh and say goodbye.

Tried navigation, lost my map,
Tangled up in a fishy claptrap.
Should I float or should I row?
I can't decide where I want to go.

As I bob along like a rubber duck,
Polishing my luck; or waiting for luck?
The waves just wobble, splashy delight,
Guess I'll ride the currents and enjoy the flight.

So here's to drifting, a heart that's free,
Swapped my anchor for a cup of glee.
If there's no land, I'll laugh and sway,
Who says the voyage can't be play?

The Mirror of Existence

Stand before the glass, say 'Boo!'
What's reflected? Is it really you?
An image of chaos, a dash of grime,
Maybe purpose is just a state of mime.

Clicking through selfies, a digital show,
Who knew existence could be so low?
"Find your truth," the gurus chant,
While I just question why no one can dance.

Parades of answers march by with flair,
Yet I'm stuck with a sock and a chair.
"Why not take a nap?" whispers my friend,
So I sign off my quest, let boredom blend.

Peering deeper, what's the surprise?
Just giggles and grins, oh such wise lies.
Turn the mirror into a paint-splashed view,
Being lost might just mean being true!

www.ingramcontent.com/pod-product-compliance
Lightning Source LLC
Chambersburg, PA
CBHW071848160426
43209CB00003B/471